W9-CBU-193

LACROSSE

AND ITS GREATEST PLAYERS

in**side** *sports*

LACROSSE
AND ITS GREATEST PLAYERS

EDITED BY MEREDITH DAY
AND ADAM AUGUSTYN

Britannica
Educational Publishing

IN ASSOCIATION WITH

ROSEN
EDUCATIONAL SERVICES

Published in 2015 by Britannica Educational Publishing (a trademark of Encyclopædia Britannica, Inc.) in association with The Rosen Publishing Group, Inc.
29 East 21st Street, New York, NY 10010

Distributed exclusively by Rosen Publishing.
To see additional Britannica Educational Publishing titles, go to rosenpublishing.com

First Edition

Britannica Educational Publishing
J.E. Luebering: Director, Core Reference Group
Anthony L. Green: Editor, Compton's by Britannica

Rosen Publishing
Hope Lourie Killcoyne: Executive Editor
Meredith Day: Editor
Nelson Sá: Art Director
Brian Garvey: Designer
Cindy Reiman: Photography Manager
Karen Huang: Photo Researcher
Supplementary material by Adam Augustyn

Library of Congress Cataloging-in-Publication Data

Lacrosse and its greatest players/edited by Meredith Day and Adam Augustyn.—First Edition.
        pages cm.—(Inside Sports)
"Distributed exclusively by Rosen Publishing"—T.p. verso.
Includes bibliographical references and index.
Audience: Grades 5–12.
ISBN 978-1-62275-592-9 (Library bound)
1. Lacrosse—Juvenile literature. 2. Lacrosse players—Biography--Juvenile literature. 3. Lacrosse players—Rating of—Juvenile literature. I. Day, Meredith, 1988– II. Augustyn, Adam.
GV989.L34 2014
796.34'7—dc23

                                                                    2014029201

Manufactured in the United States of America

CONTENTS

INTRODUCTION

The goals just kept on coming. As halftime approached in its first game of the 2014 World Lacrosse Championship in Denver, Colorado, England had surrendered six goals in a row. The other team, led by the four Thompson brothers, had spread out all over the field, making good passes and striking the ball past the goalkeeper over and over. At the end of the night, the 23 players from upstate New York, Ontario, and Quebec were victorious by a score of 15 to 4.

But these men were not competing for either the United States or Canada. Rather, they represented the Iroquois Nationals, which is the only indigenous team sanctioned to compete internationally. The Iroquois have this honor because they, along with other American Indian tribes, played the game now known as lacrosse long before Europeans came to North America. For the Nationals, many of whom grew up on Indian reservations, lacrosse is a game both physical and spiritual. As midfielder Jeremy Thompson told the *Denver Post*, "It's our way of life. It's deep in our culture. In our cradle board, we are given a wooden lacrosse stick. We grew up playing since we've been walking."

The Iroquois' 2014 victory over England was even sweeter because they had been unable to compete at the previous championship, held in Manchester, England, in 2010. The English authorities refused to grant them visas because their tribal passports were deemed a security risk, even though the U.S. government vouched for their authenticity. The Iroquois players could have traveled on U.S. passports, but they decided not to because they felt that their tribal sovereignty should be recognized internationally.

Four years later, the Iroquois Nationals had a triumphant return to the championship with a close-knit, talented team that took the bronze medal, its best showing ever. In fact, it marked

This 1847 engraving shows American Indians playing an early version of lacrosse. The game still has cultural significance for the Six Nations of the Iroquois. **SSPL via Getty Images**

the first time that a team other than the United States, Canada, or Australia finished on the podium at the World Championship. "We're competing at the highest level and I think it just gets better from here for the Iroquois Nationals," Lyle Thompson told LaxMagazine.com.

From its American Indian roots, lacrosse spread across the United States and Canada, then to England, Ireland, and Australia. It is now played around the world by men, women, and children of all ages. College lacrosse has become particularly popular, with hundreds of U.S. universities fielding strong teams and competing for national championships. Professional leagues for both field and indoor lacrosse are growing, and star athletes such as Gary Gait and Kelly Amonte Hiller have continued their record of success as coaches, too.

Read on to learn more about this exciting, fast-paced, ball-and-stick game and its most accomplished players!

CHAPTER 1

THE ORIGINS OF LACROSSE

Lacrosse is the oldest organized sport played in North America. American Indian peoples in the eastern half of the continent played an early form of the game long before European contact. The game was then much more violent than it is today; in fact, the Cherokee tribe called their version of the game "little brother of war." Some tribal contests took days to complete, featuring thousands of players and goals located miles apart. The purpose of the game, called *baggataway*, was to disable as many opponents as possible with one's stick before focusing on scoring a goal. The arduous competitions were seen as excellent training for combat, and many tribes treated them as mystic ceremonies, complete with pregame rituals and solemn dances. In some areas men and women played together, and

THE MIDDLE AMERICAN BALL GAME

Another forerunner of lacrosse was the sport known simply as the ball game, which was played by Indians throughout ancient Middle America. It originated among the Olmec people in the second millennium BCE. Then it spread to other cultures, among them the Zapotec, the Maya, the Toltec, and the Aztec. The game was mainly of a religious nature. Various myths mention it, sometimes as a contest between day and night gods. The court represented the heavens. The ball represented the Sun.

The game took place on an I-shaped court with high walls on the long sides. Players, wearing heavy padding, used elbows, knees, and hips to knock a solid rubber ball into the opponent's end of the court. In later years—after about 900 CE—the object was to hit the ball through one of two stone rings attached to the wall, one on each side of the court.

When the Spanish conquered Middle America in the 1500s, Catholic missionaries put a stop to the ball game because they disapproved of its pagan roots. A modern version of the ancient Aztec game is still played in Sinaloa, a state in western Mexico. It is called *ulama*, after the Aztec name *ullamaliztli*.

Baggataway, *the American Indian game that lacrosse is based on,* *involved many players and was considered preparation for combat.* **The Bridgeman Art Library/Getty Images**

in other areas women had their own version of the game. Indians on government reservations in the United States and Canada still field strong teams.

COMING TO CANADA

The name of the sport originated with early French settlers in Canada. Observing the

Indians play, they called the game lacrosse because the curved end of the playing stick resembled a bishop's staff, or crosier (*la crosse*). Europeans in Canada began playing the game around 1840. In playing Indian teams, white players lost so frequently that they were allowed to field extra men.

The Olympic Club, the first lacrosse organization, was founded in Montreal in 1842. In

The head of a traditional wooden lacrosse stick was shaped like the hook at the top of a bishop's staff. **Angel Wynn/Nativestock/Getty Images**

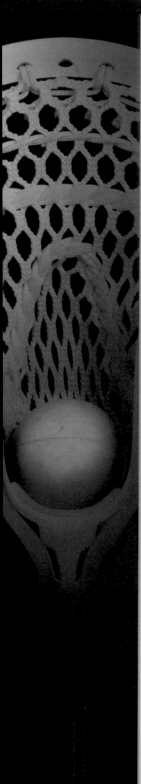

1867, the National Lacrosse Association was formed, largely through the efforts of George Beers of Montreal. Known as the "father of lacrosse," Beers set down the sport's first set of rules. He replaced the stuffed deerskin ball with a rubber one, limited the number of players per side to 12, and made modifications to the stick that made it easier to catch and throw the ball. The 12 players were designated at that time as goal, point, cover point, first defense, second defense, third defense, center, third attack, second attack, first attack, out home, and in home.

INTERNATIONAL TEAMS PICK UP THE CROSSE

From Canada, the game soon spread to England. In 1867, Captain W.B. Johnson of Montreal toured the British Isles with a team of Caughnawaga Indians. During a second tour in 1876, a game was held at Windsor Castle before Queen Victoria, who found it "very pretty to watch." The English took to the sport, and the game achieved popularity, notably in Lancashire, Cheshire, Yorkshire, Manchester, Bristol, and London. The English Lacrosse Union was founded in 1892, and the All-England

Women's Lacrosse Association was formed in 1912.

English teams exchanged visits with teams from the United States and Canada from time to time, and combined Oxford-Cambridge teams frequently exchanged visits with college or All-Star teams from the United States. The game was also introduced in Ireland, Australia, and South Africa. Lacrosse was included in the Olympic Games in 1904 and 1908 with teams representing Canada, the United States, and Great Britain, but it did not attract enough international interest to remain an Olympic sport.

SPREADING ACROSS THE UNITED STATES

In the United States, a team of Indians introduced the game in Troy, New York, around 1868. Soon, teams were formed in Troy and New York City. By the 1880s, the sport was played in a number of colleges and universities along the Eastern Seaboard, leading to the formation of the Intercollegiate Lacrosse League in 1906. The Intercollegiate Lacrosse League was reorganized in 1926 as the U.S. Intercollegiate Lacrosse Association, which had about 120 member colleges.

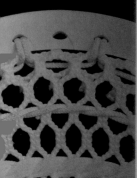

The most important step in the development and popularization of the sport came when lacrosse was introduced to Baltimore, Maryland. Baltimoreans embraced lacrosse and actively promoted the sport among all age levels, turning the city into the center of American lacrosse. Johns Hopkins University

These schoolgirls learn how to catch a high ball at the Haberdasher Aske's School in London, England, in 1939. **Fox Photos/Hulton Archive/Getty Images**

in Baltimore boasts one of the most celebrated top-division men's lacrosse programs
in the country, while all of the school's other
sports teams play in lower divisions. Johns
Hopkins is also the home of the U.S. Lacrosse
Museum and National Hall of Fame.

Although not as popular a spectator sport
as the likes of gridiron football, basketball,
and baseball, lacrosse today is widely played
in eastern schools and athletic clubs. Indoor
and outdoor men's professional lacrosse
leagues were formed in the late 20th century. The growth of National Collegiate
Athletic Association (NCAA) lacrosse programs is a testament to the growing appeal
of the sport outside of its traditional eastern
base. By 2013, there were 319 NCAA men's
teams and 416 NCAA women's teams, and
new programs continued to be added.

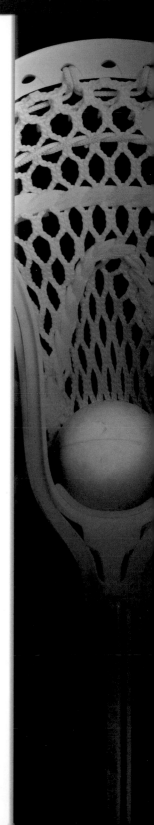

CHAPTER 2
PLAYING THE GAME

Lacrosse is played by two teams of 10 players each. It is a very fast game, the object of which is to send the ball into the opponents' goal as many times as possible and to prevent the opponents from scoring. A goal counts as one point. The men's game is divided into four periods of 15 minutes each, with intervals of two minutes between the first and second quarters and between the third and fourth quarters and a 10-minute rest at halftime. If the score is tied at the end of regulation time, play is resumed after an intermission of five minutes in four-minute overtime periods, with a one-minute rest in between. Overtime continues until a goal is scored, deciding the winner. Players can be substituted in and out of the game at any time, similar to the frequent line changes in hockey.

FIELD

For a men's lacrosse game, the field is 110 yards (100.6 meters) long and 60 yards (54.9 meters) wide. The short sides of the field are called end lines; the long sides are called side-lines. The goals, 6 feet (1.8 meters) wide and 6 feet high, are 80 yards (73.1 meters) apart—15 yards (13.7 meters) from each end line. The goal posts and the crossbar connecting them support a pyramid-shaped cord netting that slopes back to the ground 7 feet (2.1 meters)

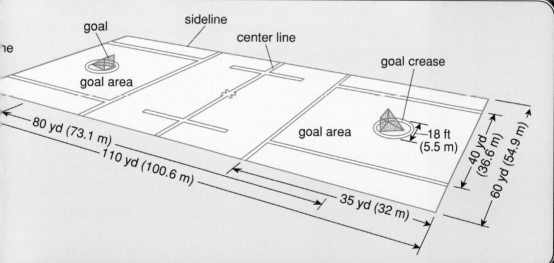

A typical men's lacrosse field. The women's game is often played on a larger field. © **Merriam-Webster Inc.**

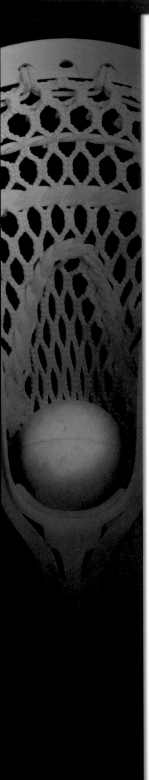

from the mouth of the goal. Around each goal is a marked circle 18 feet (5.5 meters) in diameter, known as the goal crease. Only the goalkeeper and other defensive players are allowed inside this area.

EQUIPMENT

Lacrosse is played with a rubber sponge ball 7.75 to 8 inches (19.7 to 20.3 centimeters) around and 5 to 5.25 ounces (142 to 149 grams) in weight. Each player carries a crosse, a stick shaped something like a long-handled tennis racket. In the men's game, the crosse varies in length from 40 to 72 inches (102 to 183 centimeters). The materials from which it is made also vary. While the handle, or shaft, of the crosse was traditionally made of wood, usually hickory, contemporary crosses are often made of metal or composite materials. The width of the crosse at the top, or head, must be between 6 and 12 inches (15.2 and 30.4 centimeters). The roughly triangular head has a net of gut, rawhide, cloth, or synthetic lacing, which provides a pocket to catch and carry the ball.

Each player wears a padded helmet with a wire face mask to protect himself against an accidental blow from a crosse or from a hard pass or shot. Other equipment includes thick gloves, shoulder pads and arm pads, and shoes with

LET'S SHAKE ON IT ... OR NOT

It is traditional in many sports for the team captains to shake hands before the game and for all the players to congratulate each other with a friendly handshake after the game. Lacrosse takes this ritual of sportsmanship even more seriously. A unique ceremony at the beginning of the game consists of the teams lining up in the center of the field opposite each other. Each player introduces himself to his particular opponent, shakes hands, and wishes him luck.

In 2009, some college football teams arranged pregame handshakes as part of a sportsmanship initiative from the NCAA and the American Football Coaches Association. At a Boise State–Oregon game, the players shook hands both before and after the game. However, the postgame handshake was anything but friendly. Oregon's LeGarrette Blount punched Byron Hout of Boise State, causing other coaches not to participate in the handshake ritual out of fear that it could lead to violence.

Still, many lacrosse teams continue meeting in the middle of the field before the game. Though some players say they try to intimidate their opponents with firm handshakes and aggressive looks, the handshake ritual is a respectful tradition that almost always passes without incident.

rubber or plastic cleats to assure a firm grip on the ground. The goalkeeper's equipment differs slightly from that of other players and notably includes chest and throat protectors.

WHO'S WHO

In the men's game, there are 10 players on a team: the goalkeeper, three defensemen, three midfielders (one of whom is the center), and three attackmen. During play, each team must have at least four players in its defensive half of the field and no fewer than three in its offensive half of the field. This rule prevents too many players from crowding around a goal when it is under attack.

Usually, the goalkeeper and the three defensemen stay in the defensive half, while the three attackmen stay in the offensive half. The midfielders are permitted to roam the field, reinforcing the attack or defense as needed. The goalkeeper defends his team's goal.

Three officials on the field control the game and call fouls. They include a referee, an umpire, and a field judge.

LACROSSE IN ACTION

Each quarter of play starts with a face-off in the center of the field. To begin the face-off,

In addition to the stick and ball, a helmet is crucial in lacrosse to prevent head injuries. **Haslam Photography/Shutterstock.com**

the referee places the ball between the two rival centers. At a signal from the official, each of the centers tries to get control of the ball using his crosse (stick). The center may keep it himself or bat it to a teammate. A face-off also restarts play after a goal has been scored.

The team with the ball tries to advance it toward the opponent's goal. Players may run with the ball, pass it to a teammate in any direction, and catch it, but—with the exception

of the goalkeeper—they may not touch it or another player with the hands. A player may also kick the ball or bat it. A unique feature of the game is "cradling," in which the player rapidly rotates the stick in half-turns while holding it nearly upright as he runs. The rotation keeps the ball in the pocket of the crosse and also puts it in position for accurate throwing. A goal is scored by throwing, batting, or kicking the ball into the goal.

The defenders try to force their opponents into making poor passes, intercept the ball when it is thrown, or knock the ball from an opponent's stick. They are allowed to poke the ballcarrier in the body with their sticks or slap at his stick to dislodge the ball. Blocking the ballcarrier—that is, hitting him with the shoulder in an attempt to throw him off-balance or knock him down—is legal.

Violations of the rules are penalized with technical fouls or personal fouls. Technical fouls are minor violations that result in either the suspension of the offending player from the game for 30 seconds or the awarding of the ball to the opposing team. Personal fouls are more serious offenses—for example, an illegal block. For these violations, the offender is suspended from the game for one, two, or three minutes, and his team plays a man short for that period

Geoff Snider, #17 for the Charlotte Hounds, grabs a pass intended for opponent Brent Adams in a Major League Lacrosse game. Grant Halverson/ **Getty Images**

Since body contact is prohibited in women's lacrosse, players wear goggles instead of the helmets worn by men. **Patrick Smith/Getty Images**

of time. Other personal fouls include tripping, slashing, and unnecessary roughness.

Women's Lacrosse

The rules for women's lacrosse differ in some ways from those of the men's game. The women's game allows no body contact or rough play with the stick. The stick is shorter than in the men's game, ranging from 35.5 to 52 inches (90 to 132 centimeters). There are 12 players on a side instead of 10. The field may be longer than 110 yards (100.6 meters), and the goals are 90 to 100 yards (82.3 to 91.4 meters) apart. A game consists of 30-minute halves, with a 10-minute intermission. In the event of a tie at the end of regulation time, the teams play two three-minute overtime periods. If the score remains tied at the end of those periods, play continues in six-minute periods until a goal is scored.

CHAPTER 3

LEVELS AND TYPES OF PLAY

C hildren and teenagers in the United States and Canada often start playing lacrosse in youth leagues or on high school teams. Players can then go on to compete in college, internationally, and even professionally.

YOUTH LACROSSE

According to estimates from the SFIA/Physical Activity Council, 770,000 youth between the ages of six and 18 participated in lacrosse in 2012, an increase of 158 percent since 2008. Lacrosse still lags in comparison to the team sports such as soccer and basketball, which both had over 6.5 million participants in 2012. However, it is quickly gaining popularity even as other sports decline.

THE COLLEGE SCENE

The National Collegiate Athletic Association (NCAA) has sponsored intercollegiate lacrosse

Loyola University (Maryland) men's lacrosse players celebrate a goal during the 2012 NCAA championship game, in which they defeated Maryland by a score of 9–3. **Mike Broglio/Shutterstock.com**

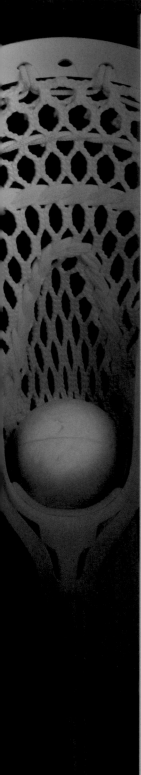

competition since 1970. NCAA national championship tournaments for men began in 1971; women's tournaments began in 1982. Syracuse and Johns Hopkins have won the most men's NCAA championships, while Maryland and Northwestern have been the most successful women's programs.

INTERNATIONAL PLAY

Separate organizations governed men's and women's international lacrosse until 2008, when they merged to form the Federation of International Lacrosse (FIL). World Championships for men have been held since 1967; only the United States and Canada have ever won. Women's World Championships were held from 1969 to 1982, when they were replaced by the World Cup. Every World Cup has been won by either the United States or Australia.

PROFESSIONAL LACROSSE

The best collegiate men's players often go on to play for Major League Lacrosse (MLL), a small professional league that debuted

Box Lacrosse

Box lacrosse, or boxla, was introduced in Canada in the 1930s to allow indoor play in places where the weather made outdoor play difficult. The games are played in hockey arenas with artificial turf in place of the ice. This means that the field is much smaller, with maximum dimensions of 200 by 85 feet (about 60 by 26 meters), with a goal 4.75 feet (about 145 centimeters) wide and 4 feet (122 centimeters) high. There are six players on a side instead of the usual 10 (men) or 12 (women). Because of the smaller playing area, box lacrosse is faster and more physical than the outdoor game, and players wear additional gear for protection.

Box lacrosse players can check their opponents into the boards that line the field. This game took place at the Air Canada Centre, which also hosts hockey and basketball. **Carlos Osorio/Toronto Star/Getty Images**

The New York Lizards and the Florida Launch are two of the teams in Major League Lacrosse. Jim McIsaac/Getty Images

in 2001. Its season runs from April to August. Another professional option is the National Lacrosse League (NLL), for box lacrosse, the indoor variant played mostly in North America. Founded in 1986, the league has its regular season from December to April, with playoffs in May. Both the MLL and NLL have teams in the United States and Canada.

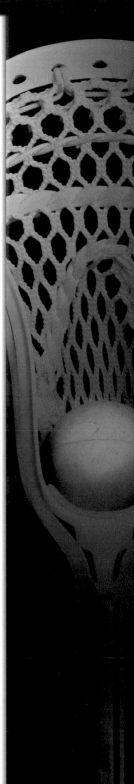

CHAPTER 4

NOTABLE PLAYERS

Though lacrosse is becoming more popular around the world, most of the elite players continue to hail from the sport's traditional hotbeds of Canada and the northeastern United States. Some of the most decorated players of the past remain involved in lacrosse as coaches.

LIONEL CONACHER

Athlete and politician Lionel Conacher was voted Canada's Athlete of the Half Century (1900–50) and was a Liberal Party member of Parliament. He was inducted as one of the charter members of the Canadian Lacrosse Hall of Fame in 1965.

Conacher dropped out of school after the eighth grade to work. His athletic career stemmed from a prize he won in 1916 for selling the most newspapers—a membership

Lionel Conacher. © The Toronto Star/ZUMA Press

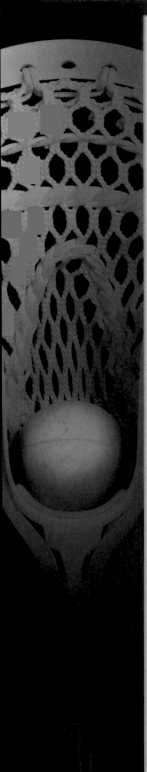

card in a YMCA gymnasium. He won the
Ontario 125-pound wrestling championship
at age 16 and the Canadian light-heavyweight
boxing championship at 20. He played on
the championship Ontario lacrosse team in
1922 and on the Toronto American Athletic
Association championship baseball team in
1926. He also played rugby for Toronto in
the Ontario Football Rugby Union (1920)
and for the Toronto Argonauts (1921–22).

Conacher's most sustained professional
sport was ice hockey. He played as a defenseman in the National Hockey League
(NHL) (1925–37) with the Pittsburgh Pirates,
the Chicago Black Hawks, the New York
Americans, and the Montreal Maroons and
was a member of Stanley Cup–winning teams
in 1934 (Chicago) and 1935 (Montreal). He
was inducted into the Hockey Hall of Fame,
posthumously, in 1994.

Conacher was elected to the Ontario leg-
islature in 1937. During World War II, he was
recreational director for the Royal Canadian
Air Force. He was elected to Parliament in
1949 and 1953. He died of a heart attack in
1954 after hitting a triple in a softball game
between members of Parliament and the par-
liamentary press gallery.

KITTY GODFREE

Though best known for her accomplishments in tennis, British athlete Kitty Godfree also excelled in lacrosse, as well as ice skating and badminton. A dominant figure in women's tennis in the 1920s, she won two singles titles at the All-England Championships at Wimbledon, five doubles titles in Grand Slam events, and five Olympic medals, including a gold in women's doubles at the 1920 Olympics in Antwerp, Belgium.

Godfree lost the 1923 All-England final to Suzanne Lenglen of France, but she returned the next year to become the only woman ever to beat American Helen Wills at Wimbledon. At the same tournament, she won the mixed doubles championship with her partner Jack Gilbert. In 1926, she repeated her feat, again winning both the singles and the mixed doubles, this time paired with her husband, Leslie Godfree. She won the U.S. championships in women's doubles (1923 and 1927) and in mixed doubles (1925). She represented England in the Wightman Cup series every year until 1934, when she retired with a 17-year career total of 46 singles and 107 doubles titles.

Godfree was also All-England badminton champion four times in the early 1920s and was a member of the national lacrosse team in 1918. She was made a vice president of the All-England Club in 1989. She died in 1992.

JIM THORPE

One of the most accomplished all-around athletes in history, Jim Thorpe was selected in 1950 by American sportswriters and broadcasters as the greatest American athlete and the greatest gridiron football player of the first half of the 20th century.

Predominantly of American Indian (Sauk and Fox) descent, Thorpe attended Haskell Indian School in Lawrence, Kansas, and Carlisle (Pennsylvania) Indian Industrial School, where he lettered in several sports, including lacrosse. While playing football for Carlisle under coach Pop Warner, he was chosen as halfback on Walter Camp's All-America teams in 1911 and 1912. He was a marvel of speed, power, kicking, and all-around ability. Also in 1912, Thorpe won the decathlon and the pentathlon by wide margins at the Olympic Games in Stockholm. In 1913, however, an investigation by the Amateur Athletic Union showed that he had

Jim Thorpe. Underwood Archives/Archive Photos/Getty Images

played semiprofessional baseball in 1909 and 1910, which should have disqualified him from Olympic competition. He was subsequently deprived of his gold medals.

From 1913 through 1919, Thorpe was an outfielder for the New York, Cincinnati (Ohio), and Boston baseball teams in the National League. He was more successful as one of the early stars of American professional football from 1919 through 1926. He spent two seasons (1922–23) with the Oorang Indians, whose owner attracted crowds by having Thorpe and his teammates dress up and perform "Indian" tricks before games and at halftime. In 1920–21, he served as the first president of the American Professional Football Association (later the National Football League [NFL]). He also excelled in such diverse sports as basketball, boxing, lacrosse, swimming, and hockey. In his later years, even as he was celebrated in magazine and newspaper articles as one of the greatest athletes of all time, alcoholism and inability to adjust to employment outside sports reduced Thorpe to near poverty. The 1951 film biography of his life, titled *Jim Thorpe—All American* and starring Burt Lancaster, transformed his story into uplifting melodrama, with the fallen hero rescued by his old coach Pop Warner.

In 1954, after his death, the communities of Mauch Chunk and East Mauch Chunk, Pennsylvania, merged to form the borough of Jim Thorpe. In 1973, the Amateur Athletic Union restored his amateur status, but the International Olympic Committee did not recognize his amateur status until 1982. Thorpe was subsequently declared a "cowinner" of the decathlon and pentathlon of the 1912 Olympic Games (along with the second-place finishers in those events). His Olympic gold medals were restored to his family in 1983.

JIM BROWN

Thought by many to be the greatest running back—if not the greatest overall player—in gridiron football history, Jim Brown was also one of the best lacrosse players of all time. Born in 1936, Brown took the sport up in junior high school and was a star midfielder at Manhasset High School in New York. He attended Syracuse University, where he lettered in lacrosse, football, basketball, and track over the course of his collegiate career. In lacrosse, Brown was named second-team All-American during his junior season and first-team All-American during his senior year, when he was second in the nation in

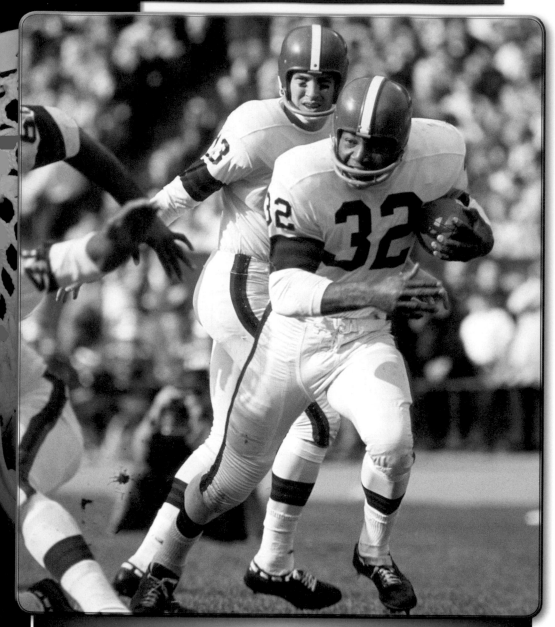

Jim Brown. **Focus On Sport/Getty Images**

scoring with 43 goals while leading Syracuse to an undefeated season.

Brown went on to a Hall-of-Fame career as a member of the Cleveland Browns of the National Football League. At 30 years of age and seemingly at the height of his athletic abilities, Brown retired from football to pursue a career in motion pictures. He appeared in many action and adventure films, among them *The Dirty Dozen* (1967) and *100 Rifles* (1969). Brown was also active in issues facing African Americans, forming groups to assist black-owned businesses and to rehabilitate gang members.

Brown was elected to the Pro Football Hall of Fame in 1971 and to the U.S. National Lacrosse Hall of Fame in 1983. He returned to lacrosse in 2012 as a co-owner of the Long Island (now New York) Lizards Major League Lacrosse franchise.

OREN LYONS

Chief Oren Lyons, Jr., is the rare lacrosse legend whose off-field exploits match—or even exceed—the wonders he accomplished with a stick in his hand. He was raised on the Onondaga Indian reservation in upstate New York. There, he learned the intricacies of the

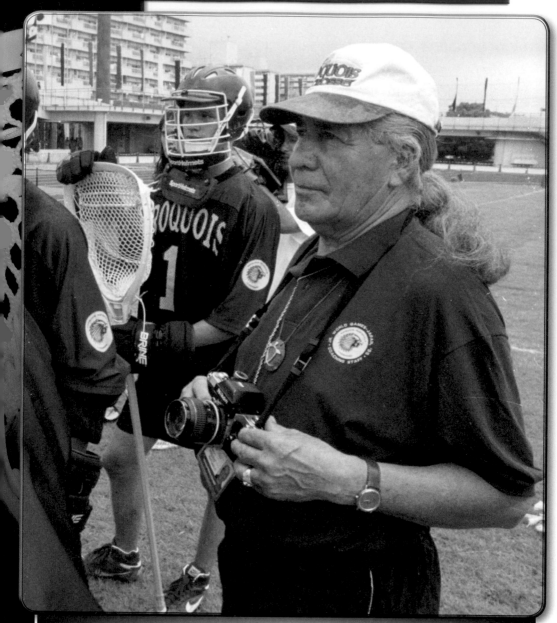

Chief Oren Lyons, Jr., stays involved in lacrosse by supporting the Iroquois Nationals at the World Lacrosse Championship.
© **AP Images**

sport by watching his father play in tribal lacrosse games. A goaltender, Lyons earned a scholarship to Syracuse University, where he was an honorable mention All-American during his sophomore season and earned third-team All-American honors in each of his final two years. He also backstopped Syracuse to an undefeated season in 1958. Though professional lacrosse did not exist in Lyons' time, he played club lacrosse for a number of teams from the time of his graduation until 1972.

Lyons became a successful commercial artist after his collegiate career ended and also was a professor of American Studies at the State University of New York at Buffalo for more than 35 years. He is a Faithkeeper of the Turtle Clan of the Six Nations of the Iroquois Confederacy and has been one of the world's best-known advocates for Native American causes. Lyons was inducted into the U.S. National Lacrosse Hall of Fame in 1992.

JIMMY LEWIS

Although small by the standards of typical lacrosse stars at 5 feet, 9 inches (1.75 meters) and 160 pounds (73 kilograms), Jimmy Lewis was nevertheless the leading player of his era.

The gritty and determined Lewis honed his skills at Uniondale High School on New York's Long Island. He led his high school team to 45 straight victories, but he was able to secure admission to the U.S. Naval Academy only after appealing to a Mississippi congressman because his home state's appointment slots were filled.

At Navy, Lewis set the NCAA lacrosse world on fire, earning first-team All-American and Attackman of the Year honors in each of his three varsity seasons, becoming the first player to win the latter award three times. (Freshmen did not play on U.S. college varsity squads at the time.) Lewis led Navy to three consecutive national championships from 1964 through 1966, during which time the team never lost a game to another collegiate lacrosse program.

Lewis did not play the sport professionally, as he went into service for the U.S. Navy once his collegiate career ended and spent 20 years as a test pilot. In 2014, he was honored with the Tewaaraton Legends Award—something of a retroactive Player of the Year award for NCAA lacrosse stars who played before the award was given out. He was inducted into the U.S. National Lacrosse Hall of Fame in 1981.

MIKE FRENCH

Like many of his countrymen, Canadian Mike French was initially a box lacrosse player. His first experience with field lacrosse came as an attackman on the freshman team at Cornell University. He quickly adjusted to the new version and was a third-team All-American in his sophomore season (1974) after leading the NCAA with 94 points (63 goals and 31 assists). He was a first-team All-American as both a junior and a senior (1975–76). In his senior year he scored 65 goals to set an NCAA Division I record for goals in a season (since broken) while leading Cornell to an undefeated season and a national championship. That year he was also named Attackman of the Year and earned the Lt. Raymond Enners Award for the most outstanding player of the year. Two years later he was the captain of Canada's first world champion lacrosse team.

With the formation of the Eagle Pro Box Lacrosse League (later the National Lacrosse League [NLL]) in 1987, French joined the Philadelphia Wings franchise and led the league in scoring. He ended his professional playing career after one season and became

the Wings' general manager in 1988. French became the franchise's executive vice president and co-owner in 1998 and assumed the role of team president in 2013. Under his executive guidance, the Wings captured six NLL titles. French was inducted into the U.S. National Lacrosse Hall of Fame in 1991 and the Canadian Lacrosse Hall of Fame in 2001, becoming the first player to earn both honors.

STAN COCKERTON

Stan Cockerton was one of the most prolific goal-scorers in NCAA history, a feat made all the more impressive by the fact that he did so while playing at North Carolina State University, a school far removed from the traditional strongholds of collegiate lacrosse. He grew up playing box lacrosse, the most popular form of the sport in Canada, but he proved his versatility when he played his first game with the field lacrosse team at N.C. State in 1977. He scored 54 times in 11 games as a freshman to lead the nation in goals. He was named a first-team All-American three times (1978–80) and in 1979 led N.C. State to the school's only appearance in the NCAA tournament. (The university dropped its lacrosse program

Stan Cockerton's son Mark (right) is an attackman for the Rochester Rattlers of Major League Lacrosse. Mark and his brother, Matt, both played college lacrosse for the University of Virginia. **Jen Fuller/ Getty Images**

in 1983.) Cockerton's 193 career goals was an NCAA Division I record until it was broken by Duke University's Zack Greer in 2008, and his 4.39 goals-per-game average remains the best mark in Division I history.

Cockerton was a member of the Canadian men's lacrosse team at the 1978, 1982, and 1990 World Championships. His overtime goal in the final of the 1978 championship gave Canada

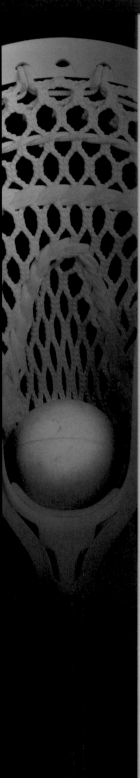

its first world title. He served as the executive director of the Ontario Lacrosse Association, and in 2010 he became the president of the Federation of International Lacrosse. Cockerton was inducted into the Canadian Lacrosse Hall of Fame in 2003 and the U.S. National Lacrosse Hall of Fame in 2014.

GARY GAIT

Along with his twin brother Paul, Gary Gait dominated lacrosse in the late 1980s and early '90s. The Gaits both played collegiate lacrosse at Syracuse University. Gary was an instant star, as he was named an honorable mention All-American in his freshman year and earned first-team All-American honors in each of the following three years. He led Syracuse to three NCAA national championships (1988–90) and two undefeated seasons (1988, 1990). Gary twice won the Lt. Raymond Enners Award for player of the year (1988, 1990). He ended his Syracuse career as the school's all-time leader in goals scored (192) and also holds the school's single-season goal-scoring record (with 70 in 1988).

Gary joined the Major Indoor Lacrosse League (later the National Lacrosse League

Gary Gait tries to score from behind the net in an NCAA game during his freshman season at Syracuse University. **Collegiate Images/Getty Images**

[NLL]) as a member of the Detroit Turbos in 1991 and was named the league's Rookie of the Year. He went on to play 17 full seasons in the NLL and a part of an 18th with seven franchises. He was named the NLL's Most

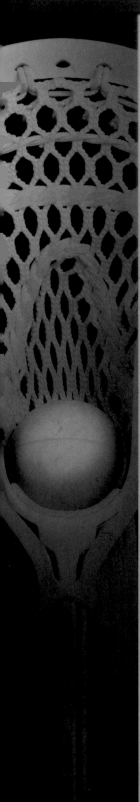

Valuable Player (MVP) a record six times (1995–99, 2003) and finished his career as the league's leading career scorer with 1,091 points (goals plus assists; the record has since been broken). Over the course of his career he captured three NLL championships: one with Detroit in 1991 and two with the Philadelphia Wings in 1994 and 1995. Gary also coached the NLL's Colorado Mammoth for two seasons, which included a championship in 2006.

In 2001, Gary began playing in Major League Lacrosse (MLL) during the NLL off-season. He spent one season with the Long Island Lizards before serving as player-coach of the Baltimore Bayhawks from 2002 to 2005. His teams won three MLL titles (2001, 2002, and 2005), and he was named the league's MVP in 2005 after leading the MLL in goals (42) and points (63).

In international play, Gary was a member the Canadian men's national team from 1990 to 2006, winning a World Lacrosse Championship in 2006. In 2012, he retired from his playing career to focus on his role as Syracuse's women's lacrosse head coach, a position he had held since 2007. He was inducted into the U.S. National Lacrosse Hall of Fame in 2005 and the Canadian Lacrosse Hall of Fame in 2014.

Gary (left) and Paul Gait during their collegiate lacrosse careers at Syracuse. **Kimberly Butler/The LIFE Images Collection/Getty Images**

PAUL GAIT

Compared to the otherworldly success of his twin brother Gary, Paul Gait had a relatively modest lacrosse career. But when compared to all other players, it becomes readily apparent that he is one of the best to ever set foot on a lacrosse field. He was a three-time All-American at Syracuse (1988–90) while helping the team

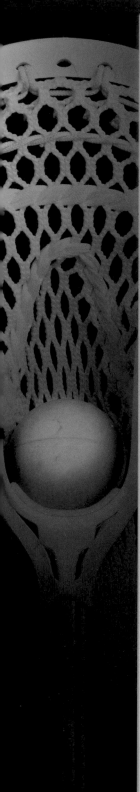

to three national championships, and he was named the Most Outstanding Player of the 1989 NCAA lacrosse tournament.

Paul joined the Major Indoor Lacrosse League/National Lacrosse League (NLL) in 1991, winning a championship with the Detroit Turbos in his rookie season. He won additional NLL titles in 1994 and 1997, and he was named first-team NLL All-Pro eight times. In 2002, he scored a career-best 54 goals in 16 games to earn NLL Most Valuable Player (MVP) honors. He played for the Long Island Lizards when Major League Lacrosse was created in 2001, and he helped the team to the league's inaugural championship that season. In international play, Paul was a four-time member of the Canadian national team at the World Lacrosse Championships. He became head coach of the NLL's Rochester Knighthawks in 2008 before moving up to the role of team vice president of lacrosse two years later. He was elected to the U.S. National Lacrosse Hall of Fame in 2005 and the Canadian Lacrosse Hall of Fame in 2014.

DAVE PIETRAMALA

One of the greatest defensemen to ever play the sport, Dave Pietramala is also the first person to win NCAA Division I championships as both a player and a head coach. Pietramala played collegiate lacrosse for the powerhouse Johns Hopkins University, where he was named a first-team All-American three times (1987–89). He was also twice the NCAA Defenseman of the Year (1988, 1989) and won the Lt. Raymond Enners Award for player of the year in 1989.

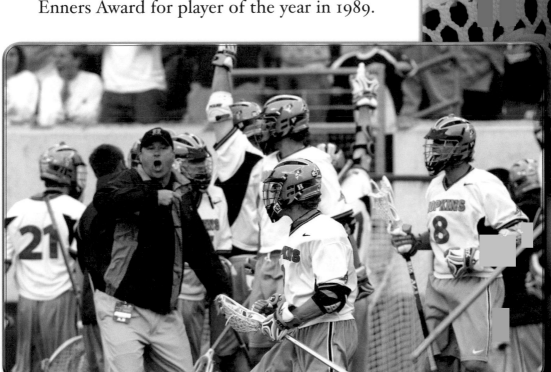

Coach Dave Pietramala (left) celebrates a goal with his players at Johns Hopkins University. **Joseph Labolito/WireImage/Getty Images**

Pietramala led Hopkins to the 1987 NCAA title and an appearance in the 1989 championship game. After college, he played at the club level and then professionally as a member of Major League Lacrosse's Pittsburgh Bulls. He was also a member of the 1990 and 1994 U.S. World Lacrosse Championship teams.

Pietramala found his calling as a coach in the early 1990s, serving as an assistant coach at various schools before becoming the head coach at Cornell University in 1997. In 2000, he guided Cornell to its first appearance in the NCAA tournament since 1995 and was named National Coach of the Year for his efforts. In the following off-season, he took over head coaching duties at his alma mater, which he led to NCAA championships in 2005 and 2007—including an undefeated season in 2005—as well as six total appearances in the lacrosse Final Four (national semifinals). In 2004, he was elected to the U.S. National Lacrosse Hall of Fame.

KELLY AMONTE HILLER

Kelly Amonte Hiller not only has a claim as one of the most outstanding female lacrosse players of all time, but she is also one of the best coaches the sport has ever seen. A member of a family full of incredible athletes—most notably brother

Tony, who played 15 seasons in the National Hockey League—she was a star lacrosse, basketball, and soccer player in high school. She attended the University of Maryland, where she was a second-team All-American as a freshman and a first-team All-American in each of the next three seasons. Amonte Hiller led the Terrapins to two national championships (1995, 1996) and earned both Defensive (1995)

Northwestern head coach Kelly Amonte Hiller (center) *gathers her team before a game against the University of North Carolina.* **Peyton Williams/Getty Images**

and Offensive (1996) Player of the Year honors. She ended her collegiate career as Maryland's all-time leader in goals (187), assists (132), and points (319). She was also an integral member of the U.S. women's lacrosse national team in 1997, 2001, and 2005, winning World Cup titles in 1997 and 2001.

Amonte Hiller spent four seasons as an assistant coach at a number of colleges before becoming the head coach of the women's lacrosse team at Northwestern University in 2000. She inherited a program that had only played at the club level before her arrival. After the team spent a year at the "elevated club" level before earning full NCAA membership, she performed one of the most remarkable collegiate coaching accomplishments in history. She quickly built the program up into a juggernaut, winning seven NCAA championships (2005–09, 2011–12) in her first 13 seasons as a head coach. She was inducted into the U.S. National Lacrosse Hall of Fame in 2012.

GREG CATTRANO

Greg Cattrano established himself as one of the best goaltenders in the history of lacrosse over the course of a career in which he was

a standout at both the collegiate and professional levels. "The Cat" was a star high school goaltender in East Setauket, New York, where he earned All-American honors and was one of the most prized recruits in the country after his senior year. He played collegiately at Brown University, where he was a second-team All-American in his junior year and a first-team All-American—as well as the NCAA Goalie of the Year—during his senior season. He finished his collegiate career with the NCAA record for goals scored by a goaltender (with three) while saving a stellar 68 percent of the shots he faced.

Cattrano first played professionally with the New York Saints of the National Lacrosse League. In 2001, he joined the Baltimore Bayhawks of the newly formed Major League Lacrosse. He was the MLL Goaltender of the Year in both 2001 and 2002, and in the latter season he also captured the MLL Most Valuable Player (MVP) award. He led the Bayhawks to appearances in the MLL title game in each of his three seasons with the team, winning a championship in 2002. Before the 2004 season, Cattrano was traded to the Philadelphia Barrage, where he won another championship (and title-game MVP honors) in his one season with the team.

Greg Cattrano.   **Doug Pensinger/Getty Images**

He also won a third MLL Goaltender of the Year award that year. He was traded to his hometown Long Island Lizards in 2005 and participated in his fifth straight MLL championship game (a loss to Baltimore, his former team). Cattrano retired in 2006 as the winningest goalie in MLL history with 40 victories and with the lowest all-time goals-against average (13.4).

JEN ADAMS

Jen Adams is widely considered the greatest female lacrosse player of all time. She was raised in Brighton, Australia, and was a member of the Australian national lacrosse team that won the 1995 under-19 world championship. She moved to the United States to attend the University of Maryland, where she established herself in the lacrosse history books and set a number of school records that still stand. Adams led Maryland to four consecutive NCAA women's Division I national titles (1998–2001) and two undefeated seasons (1999 and 2001). She finished her career as the NCAA all-time leader in career points (goals plus assists) with 445, was named a first-team All-American three times, and

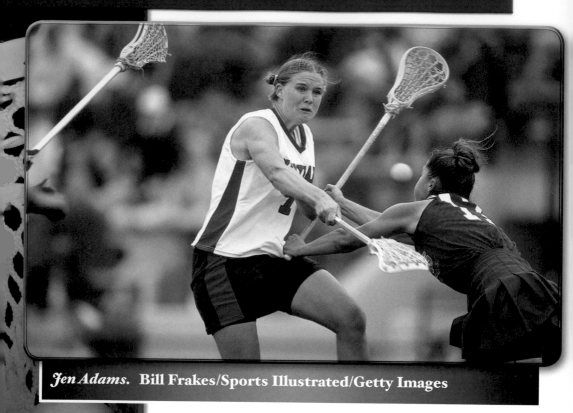

Jen Adams. **Bill Frakes/Sports Illustrated/Getty Images**

was, in 2001, the inaugural winner of the Tewaaraton Award as the best collegiate lacrosse player in the United States.

After she graduated from Maryland in 2001, Adams worked as an assistant lacrosse coach at the University of Denver and her alma mater before she became the women's lacrosse head coach at Loyola University, Maryland, in 2009. She continued to play on the international level and was a member of the Australian World Cup teams that captured a gold medal in 2005 and a silver in 2009. Adams was inducted into the U.S. National Lacrosse Hall of Fame in 2012.

MIKE POWELL

Mike Powell is the youngest and most dominant of three siblings who ruled lacrosse during the late 1990s and the first decade of the 21st century. His older brothers Casey and Ryan each set the all-time points record at Syracuse University, which was also where Mike enrolled after earning All-American honors as a high school senior. He scored 30 goals and tallied 40 assists as a freshman, leading Syracuse to an appearance in the NCAA Division I title game (an overtime loss to Princeton University). Powell became the first freshman All-American in school history that season and earned Attackman of the Year honors.

His final three seasons were even more impressive, as he captured the Attackman of the Year award in each year, becoming the first four-time winner of that award. Moreover, he won three player of the year awards (the Tewaaraton Award in 2002 and both the Tewaaraton and the Lt. Raymond Enners Award in 2004) and was first-team All-American each season. He

Mike Powell celebrates after making a big play for the Syracuse Orangemen. **Collegiate Images/Getty Images**

led Syracuse to two national championships (2002, 2004), each time earning recognition as Most Outstanding Player in the tournament, and ended his collegiate career with a school-record 307 points.

Powell joined Major League Lacrosse's Baltimore Bayhawks in 2005, helping the team to an MLL title that season. He sat out the 2006 MLL season before playing two years with the Boston Cannons. In 2008, Powell left MLL for good to pursue a music career and other interests. In international play, he was a member of the U.S. national team at the 2002 and 2006 World Championships, capturing a gold medal in 2002 and silver in 2006.

PAUL RABIL

Not only is Paul Rabil one of the best to ever set foot on a lacrosse field, but he is also arguably the first lacrosse player to achieve more wide-spread fame. A savvy businessman who works in finance when not playing pro lacrosse, he garnered a number of endorsement deals and became the face of the sport as lacrosse games began to be widely broadcast.

Rabil attended Johns Hopkins University and earned third-team All-American honors as a freshman while helping the school to an

Paul Rabil. Jim Rogash/Getty Image

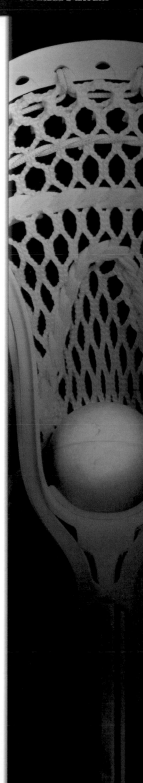

undefeated season and an NCAA national championship (2005). He was even better over the next three years, as he was named a first-team All-American each season and captured another national title with the Blue Jays (2007). He led Hopkins in scoring in each of his final three seasons and was named Midfielder of the Year in 2007. The clutch Rabil ended his collegiate career as the school's career leader in NCAA tournament goals (28), assists (23), and points (51).

Rabil was drafted by the Boston Cannons with the first overall selection of the 2008 Major League Lacrosse (MLL) draft. In 2009, he scored 33 goals in 12 games and was named both the league's Most Valuable Player (MVP) and Offensive Player of the Year. He won both awards again in 2011 as he guided the Cannons to an MLL title, and he tacked on a third Offensive Player of the Year award in 2012. During the MLL off-season he played in the National Lacrosse League, winning a league title in 2010 with the Washington Stealth.

In international play, Rabil was a member of the U.S. world championship–winning team in 2010, taking home tournament MVP honors in the process. He played again for the U.S. team in 2014, earning All-World honors.

Lacrosse has come a long way from its early days as a Native American sport that combined combat with religious ceremony. At the 2014 World Lacrosse Championship, a record 38 nations participated. Although the United States and Canada continue to dominate international competition, the game's growth worldwide is undeniable.

More and more young players are picking up a lacrosse stick and playing in youth leagues or on high school teams. As the sport's popularity increases, the level of competition in college and the professional leagues only goes up. It takes dedication to master the unique skills of lacrosse, but it's also a lot of fun. If you like a fast-paced, contact sport, lacrosse may be for you. Before you know it, you could be rushing up the field, cradling the ball in your crosse, and going for goal!

These girls are among the thousands of high school players who have discovered the fun of lacrosse. Gordon Chibroski/Portland Press Herald/Getty Images

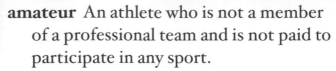

amateur An athlete who is not a member of a professional team and is not paid to participate in any sport.

arduous Marked by great labor or effort.

attackman An offensive player in lacrosse who attacks the goal and scores often.

baggataway A ball-and-stick game played by American Indians that eventually evolved into modern-day lacrosse.

cradling A maneuver in lacrosse comparable to dribbling a basketball, in which a player rotates the ball in the pocket of the stick to control the ball as he or she runs.

defenseman A lacrosse player who helps to defend his or her team's goal and prevent the other team from scoring.

face-off A confrontation between the centers on a lacrosse team that begins each quarter of play; the referee places the ball between the two players, who then compete to win possession of the ball.

goal crease A circle 18 feet (5.5 meters) in diameter around the goal that can only be occupied by the goalkeeper and defensive players.

hotbed A place or environment that favors rapid growth or development.

Iroquois Nationals The lacrosse team of the Six Nations of the Iroquois, which competes independently from the United States at the World Lacrosse Championship.

juggernaut A massive force or object that crushes whatever is in its path.

midfielder A lacrosse player who plays both offense and defense and excels in transition.

mystic Having a spiritual meaning, existence, reality, or comparable value that is neither apparent to the senses nor obvious to the intelligence.

personal foul A serious violation of the rules in lacrosse, such as illegally blocking an opponent, penalized by a suspension of one, two, or three minutes.

rehabilitate To restore a person who has committed a crime to a useful and constructive place in society.

sanction To give effective or authoritative approval or consent to.

Six Nations of the Iroquois Also known as the Iroquois Confederacy; an alliance of six Indian tribes in northern New York state (the Mohawk, Oneida, Onondaga, Cayuga, Seneca, and Tuscarora).

sovereignty A country's or American Indian nation's independent authority and right to govern itself.

technical foul A minor violation of the rules in lacrosse penalized by a 30-second suspension or losing possession of the ball.

testament Proof or evidence of the truth of something.

ulama A version of the ancient Aztec ball-and-stick game that is still played in the Mexican state of Sinaloa.